Be Mine

A VALENTINE
FOR MY
SWEETHEART

SHERYL LYNN HILL

BARBOUR
PUBLISHING, INC.

Romance, who loves to nod and sing,
With drowsy head and folded wing. . .
I have no time for idle cares
Though gazing on the unquiet sky.

EDGAR ALLEN POE

Presented to

_____

On the occasion of

_____

From

_____

Date

_____

Published by Barbour Publishing, Inc., P.O. Box 719, Uhrichsville, Ohio 44683 http://www.barbourbooks.com

 Member of the
Evangelical Christian
Publishers Association

Printed in China.

My Dearest,

When two souls, which have sought each other for however long in the throng, have finally found each other. . .a union, fiery and pure as they themselves are. . .begins on earth and continues forever in heaven.

This union is love, true love. . .a religion, which deifies the loved one, whose life comes from devotion and passion, and for which the greatest sacrifices are the sweetest delights.

This is the love which you inspire in me. . . . Your soul is made to love with purity and passion of angels; but perhaps it can only love another angel, in which case I must tremble with apprehension.

Yours forever,
VICTOR HUGO
to Adele Foucher, 1821

Love is of all passions the strongest,
for it attacks simultaneously the head,
the heart, and the senses.

VOLTAIRE

I thank my God every time I remember you.
It is right for me to feel this way about. . .you,
since I have you in my heart.

PHILIPPIANS 1:3, 7

Your Touch

Once I knew the depth where no hope was, and darkness lay on the face of all things. Then love came and set my soul free.

HELEN KELLER

Love is like a tranquil breeze that sweeps over my soul, making me whole.

UNKNOWN

Place me like a seal over your heart, like a seal on your arm; for love is as strong as death, its jealousy unyielding as the grave. It burns like blazing fire, like a mighty flame. Many waters cannot quench love; rivers cannot wash it away.

Song of Songs 8:6–7

I Miss You

I miss you even more than I could have believed; and I was
prepared to miss you a good deal. So this letter is just really
a squeal of pain. It is incredible how essential to me you
have become.

VITA SACKVILLE

*Morning without you
is dwindled to dawn.*

EMILY DICKINSON

As I mourn the idea of beginning and ending even a single day without you, I revel in knowing that this absence will not endure. In knowing. . .after this short time apart, I will once again be in your arms. The sun will shine again, and when it does, the garden within my heart will be nourished and replenished, ready to soak up the rays of sunshine you bring to my life.

UNKNOWN

I will search for the one my heart loves.

SONG OF SONGS 3:2

The Rose

I met my future husband at a Valentine's Day party. We really seemed to be drawn to each other, and the next day he called to ask where I lived. I told him, and soon he left a rose at my front door.

We began dating. At the first of each month he would leave a rose at my front door; for our one-year anniversary he left a dozen roses. Each one, he said, represented both a month, and his love. His love for me was like a rose.

The rose speaks of love silently, in a language known only to the heart.

UNKNOWN

A Red, Red Rose

O my Luve's like a red, red, rose
That's newly sprung in June;
O my luve's like the melodie
That's sweetly play'd in tune.

As fair art thou, my bonnie lass,
So deep in luve am I:
And I will luve thee still, my dear,
Till a' the seas gang dry.

Till a' the seas gang dry, my dear,
And the rocks melt wi' the sun;
I will luve thee still, my dear,
While the sands o' life shall run.

And fare-thee-weel my only luve!
And fare-thee-weel a while!
And I will come again, my Luve,
Tho' it were ten thousand mile!

ROBERT BURNS (1759–1796)

Extravagant Love

Joni Eareckson Tada tells a story of preparing for a speaking engagement while her husband, Ken, packed for a fishing trip.

As she wheeled from room to room, Joni noticed beautiful red roses in bud vases in several rooms of the house. She was surprised, and began to think that this beauty was wasteful, since neither of them would be home to enjoy the costly flowers.

As Joni left for her speaking engagement, though, the thought struck her that love is extravagant in what it is willing to give and endure.

When she returned home, another surprise awaited her: All those buds were now open, leaving a fragrant scent of love throughout the house.

How do I love thee? Let me count the ways.
I love thee to the depth and breadth and height
My soul can reach, when feeling out of sight
For the ends of being and ideal grace.

I love thee to the level of everyday's
Most quiet need, by sun and candlelight.
I love thee freely, as men strive for right;
I love thee purely, as they turn from praise.

I love thee with the passion put to use
In my old griefs, and with my childhood's faith.
I love thee with a love I seemed to lose
With my lost saints—I love thee with the breath,
Smiles, tears, and all my life!—and, if God choose,
I shall but love thee better after death.

ELIZABETH BARRETT BROWNING

You Have Touched Me Deeply

When Robert Browning met Elizabeth Barrett for the first time, she had been an invalid in her home for many years. We do not know the nature of her illness; we do know that it had for some time kept her confined to her room.

Her childhood began happily, but at age fifteen the illness and other trials took over her life. One day while Elizabeth was saddling her pony, she injured her spine.

A few years after this accident, her mother died, leaving her with eight younger brothers, two sisters, and her overbearing father—a man who wanted his children only for himself. Any suggestion of marriage for his children drove him into fury.

Robert Browning and Elizabeth knew of each other only through their published works, which fostered an admiration between them. One day Elizabeth received a letter from Robert stating, " I love your verses with all my heart, dear Miss Barrett." That note, in January 1845, began one of the greatest examples of romantic correspondence in English literature.

The following May, with the help of the maid, Robert and Elizabeth arranged a secret meeting. They continued to meet surreptitiously until September when she wrote, "You have touched me more profoundly than I thought even you could have touched me. . . . Henceforward I am yours for everything but to do you harm."

For a full year they kept meeting in secret, and writing to each other once daily—if not more often. Finally, Robert asked Elizabeth to marry him, and she said yes in spite of the difficulties the marriage would certainly face.

They eloped and were married on September 12, 1846. Out of this romantic love story, came the *Sonnets from the Portuguese*, a collection of well-known poems that have provided romantic inspiration through many generations.

*Like a lily among thorns is
my darling among the maidens.*

SONG OF SONGS 2:2

She is so encouraged. . .
by his romantic word and loving concern
for how she feels that she can't wait
to stir his heart by telling him
how much she longs for
his love and sweetness.

DICK AND CAROLE HOCKING
Romantic Lovers

Creative Romance

Some friends of ours do what they call "in-house dating." At this stage of their lives, it's difficult to get away alone. So they set up a table with a lace tablecloth, china, crystal, and candles from their wedding. One of them picks up deli food and sparkling cider. As romantic music plays in the background, they close the doors and spend several hours talking and holding each other.

Deep with us, our hearts flutter when we gaze into the eyes of the one we treasure. Our feelings may be expressed without a spoken word. With unguarded trust as its foundation, our love becomes deeper than the heart's first flutter.

I belong to my lover,
and his desire is for me.

SONG OF SONGS 7:10

A Valentine Surprise

On Valentine's Day my husband decided to surprise me. He made a miniature treasure hunt around our townhouse with clues that would lead me to different gifts. He even made a tiny map with little riddles to solve, for me to follow.

I hunted until I found all of the hidden treasures, including the most delightful of all: In the glove box of my car was a diamond ring, wrapped in a red bow and accompanied by a note that said, "I love you more than words can express. I pray this will make you feel loved and special. Love, your best friend."

How delightful is your love. . . .
How much more pleasing is
your love than wine,
and the fragrance of your perfume
than any spice!

SONG OF SONGS 4:10

Love Unfolding, A Beautiful Friendship

For a moment Anne's heart fluttered queerly, and for the first time, her eyes faltered under Gilbert's gaze, and a rosy flush stained the paleness of her face. It was as if a veil that had hung before her inner consciousness had been lifted, giving to her view a revelation of unsuspected feelings and realities. . . . Perhaps. . . perhaps. . .love unfolded naturally out of a beautiful friendship, as a golden hearted rose slipping from its green sheath.

LUCY MAUD MONTGOMERY
Anne of Avonlea

You have stolen my heart
with one glance of your eyes.

SONG OF SONGS 4:9

Best of Friends

The most romantic thing about our relationship? We developed a friendship before we were married.

I met my husband, Jerry, through a college and career group at church. I had just graduated from high school, and though I was dating someone else at the time, found that I could always talk and share freely with Jerry. When my boyfriend and I broke up, I drove to Jerry's house to give him the news. As I prepared to go home, he commented, "Who knows? Maybe some day we'll fall in love and get married." I thought he was crazy and dismissed the idea. After all, good friends don't get married, do they?

One night, several months later, he came to visit me after work. We talked about everything, it seemed, till one in the morning. As he was about to leave, Jerry asked if we could date. I agreed.

That Friday night we went out, and I felt special and secure. We got together every night for three weeks, going to a restaurant each evening, having hot tea till midnight, and talking about our dreams, goals, fears—and each other.

Three weeks later, he asked me to marry him! I was shocked, since I thought of us as "just friends." My response was, "I don't know what to say." He told me to simply say "yes." I was so touched, yet afraid, since it almost seemed too good to be true. But I soon found myself saying "yes."

We were married four months later, in early spring. Many people thought our relationship would fail, because we met and married so quickly. But I knew deep in my heart that Jerry would be my best friend for life. This year we celebrated our twentieth anniversary. I know it's possible to marry your best friend!

My dove,
my perfect one. . .

SONG OF SONGS 6:9

A Little Place in Your Heart

"Jo, I haf nothing but much love to gif you; I came to see if you could care for it. . . , that I was something more than a friend. Am I? Can you make a little place in your heart for old Fritz?"

"Oh, yes!" said Jo; and he was quite satisfied. . .how happy she would be to walk through life with him, even though she had no better shelter than the old umbrella.

LOUISA MAY ALCOTT
Little Women

Love alone is capable of uniting beings in such a way as to complete and fulfill them.

PIERRE TEILHARD DE CHARDIN

For this reason a man will leave his father and mother
and be united to his wife,
and the two shall become one flesh.

EPHESIANS 5:31

There is no more lovely, friendly, and charming relationship, communion, or company than a good marriage.

MARTIN LUTHER

Romance in a Barrel

Martin Luther, as a priest in the Roman Catholic Church, had taken a vow of celibacy. But as Luther read the Bible, he noticed that it said, "Be the husband of one wife," and determined that priests did not have to remain unmarried.

One day Luther received a letter from an unhappy young nun who lived in the convent near Grimma. She asked the young priest to help her and eleven other nuns escape their circumstances.

With the assistance of a friend, Luther devised a plan to help the nuns. The two men would hide the women in empty herring barrels, and ship them to Wittenberg.

Then a plan was devised to marry off the nuns. Luther and his friend had little trouble finding husbands for eleven of them. The twelfth nun, however, Katherine von Bora, declared she would marry no one besides Martin Luther.

Luther visited his parents, asking them what he should do. They encouraged him to marry Katherine, in part to carry on the family name. But Katherine von Bora was also a good companion for Martin Luther, and he decided to make her his wife.

On June 15, 1525, Luther and Katherine had a small private wedding. Several weeks later, the couple held a wedding feast to celebrate their happy union. And a year later, as Luther's parents had desired, the family name continued when the new couple's first son was born.

Sometimes your nearness takes my breath away;
and all the things I want to say can find no voice.
Then, in silence,
I can only hope my eyes will speak my heart.

ROBERT SEXTON

I Will

Meg looked straight up in her husband's eyes, and said, "I will!" with such tender trust in her own face and voice that her mother's heart rejoiced, and Aunt March sniffed audibly. . . . As she walked away, leaning on her husband's arm, with her hands full of flowers, and the June sunshine brightening her happy face—and so Meg's married life began.

LOUISA MAY ALCOTT
Little Women

Love's Young Dream

O the days are gone, when beauty bright
My heart's chain wove;
When my dream of life, from morn till night,
Was love, still love.
New hope may bloom,
And days may come,
Of milder, calmer beam;
But there's nothing half so sweet in life
As love's young dream.

THOMAS MOORE

Just The Beginning

We were both completely relaxed now. . . . Wynn felt it too, for he whispered softly against my hair, "This is just the beginning, Elizabeth. We have today as a memory, but we have all the tomorrows as exciting possibilities. We can shape them with hands of love to fulfill our fondest dreams."

JANETTE OKE

Satisfy us in the morning. . .
that we may sing for joy and be glad all our days.
May the favor of the Lord our God rest upon us;
establish the work of our hands.

PSALM 90:14, 17

A Romantic Proposal

One year in May, we took a family vacation to Yosemite National Park. We rented bicycles to tour the park, wanting to see as much as possible in four days.

As we rode, we came to a huge meadow with waterfalls on one side. We decided to stop and take in the beautiful sights and smells all around us.

My husband noticed a couple in the distance, and said to me, "Look, a man is on his knees, proposing to his girlfriend." I quickly grabbed our camera to capture that romantic moment, snapping off several pictures.

The man was wearing a pair of shorts and a suit coat as he knelt to propose. The woman was sitting on a blanket next to a picnic basket. After she said " yes" to his proposal, they kissed and held each other close.

A few minutes later, we decided to go over and congratulate the couple. We told them that we had taken several pictures of their romantic moment, and offered to send them copies after we developed the film. We exchanged addresses and later sent them the photographs, happy to have shared a small part in their memorable day.

Being knit together in love. . .

COLOSSIANS 2:2 NKJV

My Darling Clemmie,

In your letter from Madras you wrote some words very dear to me, about my having enriched your life. I cannot tell you what pleasure this gave me, because I always feel so overwhelmingly in your debt, if there can be accounts in love. . . . What it has been to me to live all these years in your heart and companionship no phrases can convey.

Time passes swiftly, but is it not joyous to see how great and growing is the treasure we have gathered together, amid the storms and stresses of so many eventful and, to millions, tragic and terrible years?

Your loving husband,
WINSTON CHURCHILL
January 23, 1935

The Coin

The older couple boarded the ship slowly. They were anticipating their fiftieth wedding anniversary and wanted to recapture the moment their romance had begun—on a ship to America.

As the liner pulled away from the dock, the couple sat on deck talking and watching people walk by. After several hours passed, they had dinner; but after dinner, they returned to the deck to stand in the moonlight as salty air brushed lightly past their faces.

The man pulled an old coin from his pocket. As the couple looked at the coin, memories flooded their minds. Once again they were young, standing on the deck of a ship heading for New York Harbor.

They relived the moment, fifty years before, when they had exchanged wedding vows before the ship's captain. At the end of the ceremony, the captain pulled a gold coin from his vest pocket, giving it to the couple with the words, "May God bless your love and may it be pure and solid like this gold coin. I pray you will have many happy memories together."

The man then put the coin back into his pocket as he and his wife returned to their cabin holding each others' hands.

They knew their love had been pure and solid as they had learned to give to one another, forgive quickly, and laugh at themselves—some of the things that kept their romance alive.

Kneeling by their bed that night, they thanked God for the gift of love He had given them. As they turned out the lights, they held each other close.

Grow old with me,
the best is yet to be.

Robert Browning

For my beloved wife, Elizabeth Cromwell

My Dearest,

I have not leisure to write much, but I could chide thee that in many of thy letters thou writest to me, that I should not be unmindful to thee and thy little ones. Truly, if I love thee not too well, I think I err not on the other hand much. Thou art dearer to me than any creature; let that suffice.

The Lord hath showed us an exceeding mercy: who can tell how great it is. My weak faith hath been upheld. I have been in my inward man marvelously supported; though I assure thee, I grow an old man, and feel infirmities of age marvelously stealing upon me. . . . My love to all dear friends, I rest thine.

> OLIVER CROMWELL
> Dunbar,
> September 4, 1650

*Hopeless romantics are
only hopeless in the eyes of
those who don't believe in romance.*

JEAN ZHENG

Love is something eternal—the aspect may change, but not the essence. There is the same difference in a person before and after he is in love as there is in an unlighted lamp and one that is burning. The lamp was there and it was a good lamp, but now it is shedding light, too, and that is its real function.

VINCENT VAN GOGH

Dear Josephine,

I wake filled with thoughts of you. Your portrait and the intoxicating evening, which we spent yesterday, have left my senses in turmoil. Sweet, incomparable Josephine, what a strange effect you have on my heart! . . .My soul aches with so much sorrow, and there can be no rest for your lover; but is there still more in store for me when, yielding to the profound feelings which overwhelm me, I draw from your lips, from your heart a love which consumes me with fire? Ah! It was last night that I fully realized how false an image of you your portrait gives!

You are leaving at noon; I shall see you in three hours. Until then, *mio dolce amor,* a thousand kisses; but give me none in return, for they set my blood on fire.

NAPOLEON BONAPARTE
(1769–1821)

Jenny Kissed Me

Jenny kissed me when we met,
Jumping from the chair she sat in;
Time, you thief, who love to get
Sweets into your book, put that in:
Say I'm weary, say I'm sad,
Say that health and wealth have missed me,
Say I'm growing old, but add,
Jenny kissed me.

LEIGH HUNT
(1784–1859)

John Keats lived only to the age of twenty-six. He had been diagnosed with tuberculosis when he fell in love with Fanny Brawne, the girl next door. Because of his illness, he was unable to marry. This letter, written from Rome about a year before his death, shows John's deep love and intense romantic feeling for Fanny.

Sweetest Fanny,

You fear, sometimes, I do not love you so much as you wish? My dear girl, I love you ever and ever and without reserve. The more I have known you, the more have I lov'd.

In every way, even my jealousies have been agonies of love, in the hottest fit I ever had I would have died for you. I have vex'd you too much. But for love! Can I help it?

The last of your kisses was ever the sweetest; the last smile the brightest; the last movement the gracefullest. When you pass'd my window home yesterday, I was fill'd with as much admiration as I had then seen you for the first time. . . .

*Even if you did not love me I could not help an
entire devotion to you: how much more deeply then
must I feel for you knowing you love me. . . . I never
felt my mind repose upon anything with complete and
undistracted enjoyment, upon no person but you.*

*When you are in the room my thoughts never fly out
of the window: you always concentrate my whole senses.
The anxiety shown about our love in your last note is
an immense pleasure to me; however, you must not
suffer such speculations to molest you any more; nor
will I any more believe you can have the least pique
against me.*

*Brown is gone out—but here is Mrs. Wylie; when
she is gone I shall be awake for you. Remembrances to
your mother.*

*Your affectionate,
J. KEATS*

Yes, I now feel that it was then on that evening of sweet dreams that the very first dawn of human love burst upon the icy night of my spirit. Since that period I have never seen nor heard your name without a shiver half of delight, half of anxiety. . . .

For years your name never passed my lips, while my soul drank in, with a delirious thirst, all that was uttered in my presence respecting you.

EDGAR ALLEN POE

How beautiful you are
and how pleasing,
O love, with your delights!

SONG OF SONGS 7:6